the Cost of Commitment

John White

InterVarsity Press
Downers Grove
Illinois 60515

Third printing, August 1978
© 1976 by Inter-Varsity
Christian Fellowship of the
United States of America

InterVarsity Press is the book-
publishing division of
Inter-Varsity Christian Fellowship,
a student movement active on
campus at hundreds of
universities, colleges and schools
of nursing. For
information about local and
regional activities, write IVCF,
233 Langdon St., Madison, WI 53703.

Distributed in Canada through
InterVarsity Press, 1875 Leslie St., Unit 10,
Don Mills, Ontario M3B 2M5, Canada.

ISBN 0-87784-486-0
Library of Congress Catalog
Card Number: 75-21457

Printed in the United
States of America

"Your pulse may beat more quickly when you imagine what you would do if times became difficult. But as I write, times are not difficult. We enjoy freedom unparalleled in history. What then does it mean to take up your cross when little risk is involved in following Jesus? Does his teaching about the cross have meaning only when secret police pound doors at midnight? No indeed. . . ."

To Lorrie

Contents

Suffering & the Christian

1

For years I felt guilty because I never seemed to be committed deeply enough to Christ. However much I gave up I knew I could always have given up more. My life seemed as far removed from the book of Acts as from Elisabeth Elliot's *Through Gates of Splendor*. I could not get to the kernel of Christian commitment.

One problem in particular troubled me. I had the feeling that I should be suffering more, doing without more. Yet when I did suffer, my suffering bore little relationship to my commitment. Sometimes it seemed to arise from my *lack* of commitment and at other times bore no relation whatever to it.

The cost of commitment is the price we pay for following the Way of the Cross. But you, like me, may suffer many things which have nothing to do with commitment.

I must therefore begin by excluding other forms of suffering that Christians encounter.

The Common Lot of Humanity

We suffer, as all human beings suffer, *because we are part of a fallen humanity*. We live in a world of pain. Though we know joy and beauty, though we may throw back our heads and look awestruck at the night sky, though we are moved to happiness by the call of seagulls, by the silent loveliness of coral reefs, by clean smells after rainfall or the white sweep of a ski slope, though the touch of a grandchild's hand within our palm or the memory of a winter night by a glowing stove stir contentment in us— yet all this is only half the story. The stove once burned our childish fingers. The grandchild walking beside us may have no father; the child and his mother were abandoned for alcohol. Ski slopes and coral reefs delight the rich while millions starve. Beauty and goodness, anguish and horror come mingled to us.

God does not apologize for our suffering. We may sneer at his omnipotence, his love or both. He has left us the scorching dignity of pain because he gave us real choices with real consequences. Inevitably the consequences brought tragedy on the heads of our fellowmen as well as on our own.

The woman whose child was murdered by brigands may not ask: Why did God take my baby? It was not God who killed her baby but evil men. God weeps with her.

Yet if God weeps and is almighty, why does he not intervene?

I cannot in a few sentences explain the problem of evil.

I could not explain it were I to write a whole book. God and his ways transcend my understanding. But I have a couple of pointers.

In the first place, there are things that even an omnipotent God cannot do. He cannot do them either because they are *by their very nature* impossible or else because they *violate his own integrity*. Things that are by their nature impossible are what C. S. Lewis calls intrinsic impossibilities. To say that God can create an object that is a perfectly spherical cube is not to extol his power but to talk nonsense. The words are meaningless, and as Lewis points out, to put "God can" in front of a nonsensical sentence does not turn it into sense. So to give a man freedom to choose and to act, and at the same time to deny him that freedom, is meaningless. If God gives man power to choose, then man may choose evil. And, reality being what it is, the evil can harm others.

But the matter goes deeper. The universe in which we live, spoiled though it may be by man's sinful fall, still reflects God's own nature. It is consistent with his being. And God must be true to himself. He cannot betray his own being. For instance, he cannot lie. Nor can he break his covenants.

We may see no reason why he should not so control man that wars would cease. But to do so would render man less than human and make void God's covenant with man. And even if God could do that, would any of us seriously want to be part of a race of benign humanoid computers, manipulated by a Celestial Scientist? Machines cannot suffer—yet what a price to pay to avoid suffering!

But I must leave the unfathomable mystery of why suffering exists. If we cannot fathom God's wisdom, at least we can know his heart. His response to our plight was to live among us, drinking our suffering to the dregs that he might fill up a cup of salvation for us. Soon he will write the last chapter of our history and bring in his reign of peace.

But for the present the suffering goes on. And because we Christians are human, we share with humanity toothache and heartache, broken bones and fractured friendships, degenerative diseases and social decay. Just as the sun shines on just and unjust, so bacteria invade the bodies of sinner and saint.

We Christians also suffer *from our own sins and stupidities.* When self-centeredness and pride wreck a Christian marriage, the pain is caused by sin. When a Christian teen-ager drives off an icy road at ninety miles an hour, he burns to death from his own flaming folly. If we are not immune from the common suffering of humanity, we can certainly demand no special protection from the consequences of our asinine self-will. We live in a world where fire burns. Guardian angels—yes; but asbestos-robed saints—no.

Trained by Suffering

Again, Christians suffer *by way of discipline.* If we accept God's discipline with humble, believing hearts, our lives grow purer and our faith stronger. "Count it all joy, my brethren," writes James, "when you meet various trials, for you know that the testing of your faith produces steadfastness. And let steadfastness have its full effect, that you may be perfect and complete, lacking in nothing" (Jas. 1:2-4).

To grasp the secret of disciplinary suffering is to experience a transformation. Your bewilderment and dismay turn to joy. Strength makes resolute your enfeebled limbs and a song rises in your throat. "For the moment all discipline seems painful," notes the writer to the Hebrews; "later it yields the peaceful fruit of righteousness to those who have been trained by it" (Heb. 12:11).

To those who have been trained by it. . . . Trained by suffering? How? And how do I know whether the suffering has come because of my own sin or because God is teaching me?

I may not always know. And in any case, the cause matters relatively little. What matters is my reaction to suffering. For I may be "trained by" suffering without understanding fully the reasons giving rise to it.

To be trained by suffering I must have faith in God. He is still the active Ruler of the Universe. He is still my Heavenly Father.

He knows what I suffer and he cares.

For all of this I must thank and praise him. Moreover, in a way that defies analysis, God is able to bring good out of evil. He awaits only my confidence in him to turn suffering into a knife to carve away moral cancer. As drought in summer makes tree roots dig deeper into the soil or as exhausting training increases the power and speed of an athlete, so suffering makes saints.

In suffering then, I give thanks. I give thanks not *for* the suffering (God is not training me in masochism) but *in* it. I thank him that his grace is sufficient. I thank him that he is well able to deliver me and that in his own time he will. I thank him that he can turn the suffering to serve his own purposes in my life. I thank him that because Jesus, as man, suffered more than I ever will, God understands how I feel from personal experience.

And as I praise and thank him I become aware of two things. The suffering lessens. It lessens because the anxiety and fear that accompanied it have gone. (Peace in suffering halves its intensity.) In addition, hope is born as well as a sense of *meaning* in the suffering. I become almost excited that it will turn to my good. No longer do I wonder how I can bear the suffering. Suffering becomes a sort of chariot on which I ride to new planes of living.

For Jesus' Sake
In this book, however, I shall not be talking about suffering we share with all humanity, nor suffering arising from our own stupidity and sin, nor yet disciplinary suffering. When I speak of Christian suffering, I am referring to that suffering I experience *because of my loyalty to Christ.* I do not even mean suffering because of the way I witness (some of us suffer because we are obnoxious and self-righteous) but suffering that arises because I stand close to the suffering Christ.

Christian suffering has to do with the cross I take up and heave on my back. It is suffering because of a deliberate choice. The kind of cross to which Christ refers is not a "cross" of rheumatism or of the petty annoyances that older evangelicals used to label their "cross in life." It is the badge of a true follower of Jesus. It may take any form—sickness, hunger, loneliness, persecution, death. It has been the glory of the church for two thousand years. And to all who read this book, the words of the Lord of the church come ringing across the centuries: "Be faithful unto death, and I will give you a crown of life" (Rev. 2:10).

Jesus & Suffering

How did Jesus feel about the suffering he was to encounter? When did he first realize he faced death?

We don't know. We don't even know when he grasped who he was. He seemed as a child to sense a special calling and that he "must be in my Father's house" (Lk. 2:49). Yet possibly it was not until he underwent baptism in the River Jordan that a realization broke over him that a cruel death awaited him.

The Baptism of Jesus

The baptism of Jesus marked the beginning of his public ministry and perhaps his first premonition of horror ahead. It was therefore a turning point in his life.

His cousin John the Baptist recognized that Jesus did not need to repent of his sins (which baptism by John was all about) and refused to carry it out. But Jesus overcame John's reluctance with the strange words, "Let it be so now; for thus it is fitting for us to fulfill all righteousness" (Mt. 3:15).

How are we to understand these words? What did he mean by "fulfilling all righteousness"?

Three explanations are possible, two of which we will reject immediately. The third, if it is true, gets near the heart of Jesus' attitude to suffering.

The most obvious explanation is that Jesus, like others in the crowd, felt he had something to repent of. Pure as his life was, his keen conscience was troubled by something that might mean nothing to us but which he with higher ethical standards wished publicly to own as sin. In this way he would set us an example of repentance.

Such a view clashes with what Jesus elsewhere said about himself. It also contradicts what other New Testament writers teach. "Which of you convicts me of sin?" Jesus later demanded of a hostile crowd in the temple (Jn. 8:46). The writer to the Hebrews declares to us that Jesus "in every respect has been tempted as we are, *yet without sinning*" (Heb. 4:15). The New Testament rejects any idea of moral imperfection in Jesus. Jesus was not repenting of anything when he got John to baptize him.

A second explanation has to do with baptism itself. Some preachers, trying to persuade people to get baptized, say he was baptized as a "good example" for us. We are supposed to be baptized because Jesus was.

Yet when a Christian is baptized he is saying something very different from what John's converts were saying when they were baptized. In those days to be baptized was to identify yourself with the person and teaching of the one in whose name you were baptized. By being baptized you were saying, "I want to follow this man's teaching." There is no virtue in the act itself. The whole point of Christian baptism is that you *align yourself openly with Jesus.* It is an outward confession of your inward commitment to him.

The Meaning of Jesus' Baptism

What then was Jesus declaring by being baptized with John's baptism? In the first place he evidently saw it as something God the Father wanted him to do. This would seem the most obvious interpretation of his words, ". . . it is fitting for us to fulfill all righteousness." Again, his action clearly declares that he approved John's preaching. But perhaps most important of all it marks his willingness to *identify himself with sinful mankind.*

He identified with us *in the dilemma of our sin.* He placed himself where we were. He became our champion by standing in line with us. In Matthew, Luke and John he is seen up to this point as the holy Son of God. From this point on he refers to himself also as the Son of Man. The distinction is important: if he was to die as our representative and substitute he must be both. Only as the Son of Man could he represent us. Only as the Son of God could he redeem us.

Yet the step he took is of more than theological interest. It reveals his willingness to suffer. As we think about it we are brought up against the wonder of the gospel story. What began with his Incarnation he here confirms by a second deliberate choice.

And the Incarnation is amazing enough. Think of God as a diapered baby in a manger. The mind that created the universe is now limited to the body of a human infant. When God is hungry he cannot even ask in a dignified manner to be fed. He must cry like any other baby and move his little limbs, aimlessly opening and closing tiny fists. His toilet needs must be looked after by others. Angels and demons must have shaken their heads in wonder.

Modern politicians go through empty motions pretending to identify themselves with their constituents. God the Son became in very deed one of us. He could not possibly have been more human. He did not arrive on the scene as a fully formed adult male. He shared all the experiences we humans encounter of both intra-uterine and extra-uterine life. And at the outset of his public ministry he again humbles himself as he stands in line with the rest of us.

I am reminded of an experience I had as a medical student. I had missed one of the clinical sessions at a treatment center for venereal diseases. To make up for lost time I was obliged to go to the clinic at night, when medical students did not normally attend. As I entered the door, a strong male nurse took me by the arm and pushed me into a line of shabbily dressed men awaiting treatment.

"Excuse me, I've come to see the doctor in charge," I tried to explain.

"So have all the rest," the nurse replied. "Wait your turn."

"You don't understand. I'm a medical student."

"That's all right, sonny, medical students get it the same way as everyone else."

Eventually I got him to understand that I was part of the treatment team, not a patient. But I had learned something. I had learned how huge was the chasm between "us" and "them" and how unwilling I was to cross that chasm and identify myself with patients suffering from V.D. I have since then been filled with wonder at the chasm Jesus (who knew no sin) crossed to stand beside us sinners, waiting to be baptized.

And it was in response to this action, an action by which he willingly shared our humiliation, that two things occurred. First, the Holy Ghost in the form of a dove (visible at least to John the Baptist and probably to others) descended and rested on Jesus. Second, a voice from heaven was heard to declare "This is my beloved Son, with whom I am well pleased" (Mt. 3:17).

The sentence combines two quotations from messianic passages in the Old Testament, one in the Psalms and the other in Isaiah. One announces his sonship, the other his approaching suffering. Psalm 2 has to do with the power and triumph of the Lord's anointed one. From this psalm come the words, "You are my son" (Ps. 2:7).

Isaiah 42, on the other hand, is one of the servant passages in Isaiah, the most famous of which is Isaiah 53. From Isaiah 42:1 come the words "in whom I am well pleased" or "in whom my soul delights." Taken as a whole, the servant passages in Isaiah give a picture of a faithful servant who will establish righteousness and suffer death, redemptive death, in the process. While Isaiah 42 does not speak specifically of Messiah's death, there is little doubt in my mind that Jesus was aware of what the quotation implied. He himself chose this passage and read it in the synagogue at Nazareth, claiming it referred to him (Lk. 4:18-21). And if he was aware that the servant passages referred to him, he would be aware at the time of his baptism that he faced suffering and death (Mt. 3:17).

And even if I am mistaken about the words spoken from the skies, it is clear that at a later date Jesus had a vivid grasp of the death he would face. When Peter made his famous confession, "You are the Christ, the Son of the living God" (Mt. 16:16), we read that "from that time Jesus began to show his disciples that he must go to Jerusalem and suffer many things . . . and be killed and on the third day be raised" (Mt. 16:21). He was careful to establish in the minds of the disciples the connection between his divinity and his approaching sacrifice. He was the beloved Son, but he was also the suffering servant.

It is important then, as we pursue an understanding of Christian suffering, to inquire what attitude Jesus had to suffering. As we do so, four things stand out: (1) the ferocity with which he rejected any suggestion that he avoid suffering for our redemption, (2) his avoidance of *needless* suffering, (3) his teaching about the paradox of throwing life away only to find it, and (4) his insistence that what was true for him applied equally to every follower of his.

Jesus' Stern Rebuke to Peter

Poor Peter. His confession of Jesus as Christ had been received warmly.

"Blessed are you, Simon Bar-Jona! For flesh and blood

has not revealed this to you, but my Father who is in heaven" (Mt. 16:17). Peter must have felt both excited and happy. It was only human of him to protest when Jesus stated he must suffer and die. Jesus, always compassionate, might have been expected to correct him gently.

His actual words shake us: "Get behind me, Satan! You are a hindrance to me; for you are not on the side of God, but of men" (Mt. 16:23).

Jesus could not have expressed his feelings in stronger terms. Much more is involved than his relationship to Peter, for when Peter, later on, denied Jesus with oaths and cursing, Jesus treated him only with tenderness and love. His shocking response to Peter's protest, then, represents a reaction to the idea Peter expressed. Peter had unwittingly touched on something about which Jesus felt very deeply.

Could Jesus already have felt himself shrinking from the suffering that awaited him? He was human, remember, as well as divine. Did he battle deep in his heart to resist an urge to choose an easier, more comfortable path? Certainly in the Garden of Gethsemane he cried out to the Father in anguish to show him if there was any other way his mission could be accomplished (Mt. 26: 36-46). Another time he cried out, "Now is my soul troubled, And what shall I say? 'Father, save me from this hour'? No, for this purpose I have come to this hour" (Jn. 12:27).

Suffering was no easier for Jesus to face than it is for us. He who "set his face as a flint to go to Jerusalem" had to overcome every human instinct and resolutely choose a pathway of suffering and death. The ferocity of his pro-test was a measure of the internal conflict he faced. Tempted in all points as we are, he was also tempted to choose an easier way. But he recognized the temptation as satanic and one he had first faced in the desert. He sensed the treachery of the manhood he had assumed, a manhood which clung to life. He felt the powerful God-given instinct of self-preservation and overpowered it by an even stronger resolve. Hence the ferocity of his retort.

Jesus' Avoidance of Needless Suffering

In the eleventh and twelfth chapters of his Gospel, John records an interesting sequence of events. Jesus had cre-ated a sensation by raising Lazarus from the dead. The tide of Christ's popularity was running so strong that in an emergency meeting of the Sanhedrin, Caiaphas the High Priest made it plain that Jesus must die. As Caiaphas saw it, the death of Jesus would mean that the Jews would avoid trouble with their Roman rulers. His suggestion quickly turned into serious planning (Jn. 11:45-50).

Jesus was aware of the danger and deliberately sought temporary obscurity in Ephraim on the edge of the desert. He was not interested in suffering for the sake of suffering. On another occasion when a mob wanted to lynch him, Jesus slipped out of their grasp.

If Jesus was resolute in facing death on some occa-sions, he was equally quick to avoid it on others. Why? Was he stronger on some days than others?

The New Testament never suggests that sacrifice and suffering are in themselves good. Jesus faced the cross because it was the only way sinners could be redeemed.

He "endured the cross, despising the shame" (Heb. 12:2), not because it was virtuous to do so but because suffering and death were the price he had to pay to achieve his purpose.

This is important. Religious teachers down the ages have taught ascetic techniques, sometimes because making yourself suffer heaps up merit points for you but more often as a kind of Spartan training by which you subdue your rebellious body to a point where you can be truly spiritual. Such suffering is found nowhere in the life of Jesus. Although he was poor, there is no suggestion of asceticism in his whole life. Indeed he was accused of being "a glutton and a drunkard" (Mt. 11:19), simply because, as he himself acknowledged, he ate and drank like any other man of that day. If he fasted or spent time in prayer, he had a purpose in doing so. He was not training himself to subdue his bodily appetites.

The life of Jesus is totally free of both attitudes to suffering. When finally he faced his passion, it was because "the hour" was come. Jesus was not a masochist, a Spartan, nor an ascetic. He faced suffering and death because he loved lost human beings and because there was no other way he could save them.

The Paradox of Life from Death
Although Jesus was aware enough of the danger of his position to avoid running unnecessary risks, he eventually made a public entry into Jerusalem. Passover crowds were seized with a wild surge of enthusiasm. Cloaks and palm leaves were strewn on the roadway as he approached the city riding a young ass (Jn. 12:9-19). Some

of the sensation doubtless went back to the incident in Bethany where Jesus had raised Lazarus from the dead. In the temple, even foreign visitors were inquiring after him (vv. 20-22). A lesser man might have become intoxicated enough with popular acclaim to try to ride to power on the crest of the wave. But when Philip brought Jesus the message that Greek visitors were inquiring after him, he responded with an ecstasy of a different kind.

"The hour has come for the Son of man to be glorified" (v. 23), he said. Did he mean that he had it made? Did he feel there was enough popular support for him to swing an armed revolution? The words that follow dispel any such idea: "Truly, truly, I say to you, unless a grain of wheat falls into the earth and dies, it remains alone; but if it dies, it bears much fruit" (v. 24).

To be glorified, then, is not to ride popularity to a position of power but to give one's life fruitfully.

Jesus is going to win power not by grasping for it but by laying down his life for others. Indeed throwing away one's life is the only way to find it. "He who loves his life loses it, and he who hates his life in this world will keep it for eternal life" (v. 25).

By weakness and defeat
He won the mead and crown—
Trod all His foes beneath His feet
By being trodden down.[1]

We have already seen however that Jesus is not teaching that suffering is in itself virtuous. He did not pursue suffering as an end in itself. His conduct was guided by a dual principle—obedience to the Father and love for mankind. Both principles demanded that when the time was ripe he must face the cross. However painful it might prove and however much he would shrink from it in aversion, he was determined (in submission to the Father and in love to man) to face all it involved—to be the corn of wheat and fall into the ground and die. He was ready to hate his own life.

To "hate" in this context means to value something else infinitely more than life. Faced with a choice between preserving your life and obeying God you choose obedience. You choose it because your relationship to God is more important than life. Jesus did not hate his life out of bitterness or depression. He hated it in the sense that he *scorned the idea of clinging to life* when so much else was at stake.

But there could be different reasons for his willingness to face death. Schweitzer and others have suggested that Jesus welcomed the thought of the cross for psychological reasons. Believing himself to be Messiah and yet perceiving that he must inevitably be defeated in a conflict with Jewish and Roman authorities, Jesus resolved the tension between external reality and inner conviction by seeing himself as the sacrificial Lamb of God. In this way he did not have to give up his belief in his divinity but could go happily to his death believing himself to be the savior of the world.

There is an a priori assumption in this view. It is that Jesus was only man; that he was not in fact God Incarnate. It is assumed that he is man, struggling and growing in an attempt to understand God as well as to understand his own person and the human dilemma. The solution at which he eventually arrives is forged in the stress of bewildering circumstances. It is also a psychotic solution. No one would say this, but it makes Jesus out to be a crazy man.

If, however, Jesus is indeed God, the whole picture changes. No complex theory of Christ's internal resolution of stressful problems is necessary. Why then do I mention the view? I mention it because some of us may in fact give way to suffering because at times it is easier to do so than to face misunderstanding or inter-personal difficulties. Suffering can at times be an escapist solution. Theologians have probably read into the actions of Jesus psychological weaknesses of their own.

For instance, this morning in our hotel the waiter had served my wife's breakfast but not mine. I had been served orange juice and coffee but nothing else. "Signal to him," my wife said, "don't just sit there." However, I had seen how busy the waiter was and had observed other guests treating him rudely. I was reluctant to create a fuss. Yet if I am honest, I have to confess that my reluctance did not arise from consideration for the waiter but from simple cowardice. I didn't want the waiter to feel sore at me. I was willing to give up my breakfast rather than offend him.

Now I suppose I could have fooled myself into believing I was being spiritual. I was sacrificing my rights. I was being a "doormat for the Lord." But to do so would be to do precisely what some theologians maintain that Jesus did when facing the cross—take the psychologically easiest course. As a matter of fact I got up from the table, went over to the waiter and politely told him of his mistake.

Jesus never dodged tough issues, and he never taught his followers to do so. He faced embarrassing issues squarely, and on one significant occasion, violently. Jesus will not countenance "suffering" under the guise of spirituality when such suffering is in fact an escape from an embarrassing situation.

Jesus was altogether healthy in his attitude to sacrifice and suffering. He hated them. He shrank from them. Yet he chose them deliberately because there was no other way to redeem us. And his motivation in choosing death was that he anticipated joy and triumph beyond it: "who for the joy that was set before him endured the cross, despising the shame" (Heb. 12:2). In his brief talk to Philip in John 12, Jesus makes no bones about the fact that the corn of wheat that fell into the ground and died *brought forth much fruit*. There was no other point in being a corn of wheat. He also made it very clear that a general principle is involved—namely that by holding one's life lightly, by seeking the will of God above life itself, one learns the qualitative difference between existence and true and eternal living. By facing death one starts to live.

It is sentimental to view the crucified Jesus as a lovely model of passive anguish. In truth he is an active conqueror, grappling powerfully with sin and death. He is our champion, scorning his own life that he might batter down the prison doors and set captives free.

He Hell, in Hell laid low.
Made sin, He sin o'erthrew
Bowed to the grave, destroyed it so
And death, by dying, slew.
Bless, bless the Conqueror slain!

Slain in His victory!
Who lived, Who died, Who lives again
For thee, His Church for thee![2]

There is nothing morbid about the sacrifice of Jesus.
The music of the Passion must be written in a major, not
a minor key. He looked on the travail of his soul and was
well pleased. He saw beyond his death to the army of the
redeemed, drawn to him in salvation when he was lifted
up. And though he sweat great drops of blood, though he
knew spiritual and physical agony, his death was the
death of a strong man binding the god of this world. We
speak of him as the Lamb of God to remind ourselves
of his purity, not of his passivity. We do well to remember
that he is also the Lion of the tribe of Judah.

Following Jesus

The principles which were true of Jesus must also be true
of you if you wish to follow him: "If any man would come
after me, let him deny himself and take up his cross daily
and follow me" (Lk. 9:23). I shall devote the rest of the
book to dealing with this monumental principle. But as
we come to the end of the chapter, let me enunciate the
basic principle of interpretation and summarize what I
have said so far.

In the first chapter I defined Christian suffering to
exclude three types of suffering: the common suffering
all men are exposed to because we live in a fallen world;
the sufferings that arise from our own sin and stupidity;
and disciplinary sufferings, those painful experiences by
which we grow in faith and in grace. I limited Christian
suffering to that suffering which arises as one of the

direct consequences of following Jesus Christ closely.

The distinctions I have made may be a little artificial. For instance, painful experiences that arise from my own stupidity can contribute to my spiritual growth. If I respond to them appropriately, I can learn from my mistakes. Again, pain that comes to me as a result of my being close to Christ can have the same beneficial results in my life. Nevertheless the distinction is important since before deciding to follow Christ closely I must count the cost. I must recognize that in some sense I face death all the time.

I must also recognize that the attitudes that Jesus had to suffering will serve as a model for me as I face suffering too. He faced redemptive suffering with fierce resolve, seeing as satanic anything that would turn him aside. But he saw no virtue in suffering for suffering's sake, and he avoided it where possible. Moreover his outlook on suffering was not morbid, neurotic or masochistic. He saw beyond the pain to glory and victory. And it was the prospect of glory to the Father, of salvation to mankind and of victory over darkness that impelled him to overcome the shrinking of his flesh and to march forward resolutely, trampling death under his feet.

We are invited to walk in the steps of a conqueror.

Take Up Your Cross

I cannot stress strongly enough that there is no virtue in suffering itself. It makes no sense to choose to suffer when you don't have to. You prove nothing by lying across a railroad track and letting the train amputate one of your legs. But if in rescuing a child from peril you lose a leg, then the amputation, disastrous as it may be, constitutes a badge of sacrificial courage and a reminder of the value of a human life. Such suffering has merit.

When Jesus tells you to take up your cross daily, he is not telling you to find some way to suffer daily. He is simply giving forewarning of what happens to the person who follows him. The phrase has no mystical significance. It is neither a call to seek suffering as an end in itself nor an invitation to undergo an inner experience of dying.

True, you will "die" to your own ambitions, your own pathway in life, if you resolve to follow Christ, but it is not to such a death that Jesus refers. "If you want to follow me," he is saying, "be prepared for what you will have to face. They put me on a cross—and they may do the same to you. They ridiculed me—they will ridicule you. You will do well, then, to arm yourself daily with a willingness to take whatever may come to you because of me."

In the Gospels Jesus makes the point a number of times. "Behold, I send you out as sheep in the midst of wolves," he told the disciples; "so be wise as serpents and innocent as doves. . . . You will be hated by all for my name's sake. . . . A disciple is not above his teacher, nor a servant above his master. . . . If they have called the master of the house Beelzebub, how much more will they malign those of his household" (Mt. 10:16-25).

Again, in his last discourse to the apostles: "Remember the word that I said to you, 'A servant is not greater than his master.' If they persecuted me, they will persecute you. . . . All this they will do to you on my account" (Jn. 15:20-21).

Jesus does not urge his followers passively to accept any persecution that comes their way. "When they persecute you in one town, flee to the next," he tells them in Matthew 10:23. In the context in which it is found, "Take up your cross" means something similar to "Take your life in your hands" or "Be prepared to carry your own noose around with you—to run the risk of anything, even death itself. Don't seek death. Avoid it if you can, and get the gospel message to anyone who will listen. If men threaten you, go someplace else where they will listen."

Living as we do in an age of tolerance and political freedom, we forget the risks many Christians have run in other times and places. Today in Eastern Europe, Cuba, Russia, China and parts of the Muslim world, faithfulness to Christ costs. To us the plight of our brothers and sisters may seem remote. We should remember that the degree of tolerance and freedom we know are unparalleled in world history. As little as fifty years ago there was less religious toleration than exists in the West today. Yet already grave signs are apparent.

The crucifixion of Jesus set in motion a chain reaction of harassments, imprisonments and martyrdoms for his followers that has continued to this day. In most parts of the world for most of the past two thousand years followers of Christ have risked imprisonment and death. At times Christians have gone to their deaths by thousands, and have done so singing the praises of the Lamb upon the throne.

It would be foolish of us to assume that our present luxurious freedom will continue indefinitely. (Freedom is the delayed end result of the Reformation, with its biblical view of man. As the biblical influence wanes, it is likely that freedom will not continue.) There are signs that the conditions necessary for tolerance and freedom are already being eroded. Democracy is a fragile flower of late bloom (it was in its present form completely unknown to the Greeks) liable to be withered by scorching winds of impatient hate.

It is therefore important that we all ask ourselves: Am I willing to risk imprisonment and death for Christ? Many professing believers are not willing. As tyrannical and anti-religious regimes (both left- and right-wing) have sprung up around the world in the twentieth century, prominent Christian leaders and established Christian institutions living under them have shown too great a readiness to "cooperate" with Caesar. On the other hand an uncooperative minority has found itself stripped of the civil liberties we take so much for granted.

Where would you stand if you had to face what Christians faced in Nazi Germany in World War II . . . or more recently in China and Cuba? The invitation is subtle. No one is asked to renounce Christ—only to put him in his proper place, second to People and State. The pressure is fierce. "Perhaps if I cooperate from within, I will be able to influence them more" is the argument of many. The church in the first century was exposed to similar temptations. In such a world Christ calls you as he called them to pick up your noose daily and follow him.

If you are faithful in little things while freedom lasts, chances are that you will be faithful when the big tests come. There is valuable training in faithfulness where you are now. If you are open and honest—true to yourself and true to Christ—your life will provoke hostility in some and will powerfully attract others. To some it will be "a savour of life unto life" and to others "of death unto death". If you are faithful to him it may make you unpopular and unprosperous. (Of course it may have the opposite effect too. The question is: Do you, in fact, put Christ first whether it costs you or not?)

I do not wish to be an alarmist about what it costs to be faithful to Christ. Yet I feel I must point both to Scripture and to the course of church history. I want to awaken the

Western church with the blast of a trumpet, warning her that the normal conditions under which the church bears witness are not those we now experience, but are conditions inimical to Christian witness. I believe that the darkness may be descending again, and I fear that few of us are prepared for it. We belong to a long tradition of martyrdom, but we have become soft and ill-prepared.

"*Do not be surprised,*" writes Peter, "*at the fiery ordeal which comes upon you, . . . as though something strange were happening to you.* But rejoice insofar as you share Christ's sufferings that you may also rejoice and be glad when his glory is revealed. . . . If one suffers as a Christian, let him not be ashamed, but under that name let him glorify God" (1 Pet. 4:12-13, 16).

Peter gives three reasons why we should be happy to suffer for Christ. In the first place we should rejoice because we are sharing his sufferings with him. We should also be glad because we will share in his glory. Finally, suffering is a sign that God's Spirit is manifest in our lives.

Sharing Christ's Suffering

We cannot call our suffering for Christ's sake "redemptive." We are not taking on their behalf the suffering *other people* deserve. Yet there is a sense in which we are suffering for the sake of our fellowmen. We are suffering so that they might see and know Christ. In this way we share the sufferings of the One who hungered, experienced weariness, was mocked, maligned and spat upon, all because he sought to help his persecutors. Whenever his followers experience the same hostility or the same hardships for the same reason, they are truly sharing

Christ's suffering. We walk with him, and the abuse that falls on him falls also on us.

And this sharing creates new bonds. Read *Foxe's Book of Martyrs* (if you can stomach it) or Merle D'Aubigne's *History of the Reformation* and you will be astonished at the buoyant rejoicing of persecuted Christians in former ages. Their joy amazes us. Tortures that would have reduced us to jabbering idiots left them still praising God. We cannot see ourselves showing anything like the same temerity and fortitude.

What we fail to realize is that to share Christ's sufferings is also to draw near to him. And to draw near to him, be the outward circumstances what they may, is to be filled with joy. Like Stephen as rocks battered his fragile frame, we see heaven opened and know that things are not what they appear to be. In such circumstances it becomes easy to pray for one's enemies.

Christians will never go through the black night Christ passed through. That passage was for him alone. And even those parts of his suffering we *are* privileged to share are those in which we shall enjoy his nearness. We need have no fear of them.

Sharing Christ's Glory

I pointed out earlier that when Christ suffered, his eyes were fixed on "the joy that was set before him." He looked forward to "bearing much fruit." In the same way Christians must look beyond suffering to the glory that awaits them. If we suffer with him, we shall also reign with him.

Some halo hunters feel it ignoble to be concerned

about rewards when they suffer for Christ. They tell us it would be more spiritual to suffer without any thought of reward. After all Christ has done for us, no suffering is too great to undergo for him.

True. Yet if he offers reward, who among us will turn up his nose at the magnanimity of the King of Glory? And since the Scripture records such promises for our encouragement and hope, why not keep the promises before our eyes lest the day of testing throw us?

Rewards in Scripture are promised for all forms of faithfulness, but especially for faithfulness in suffering. We do not fully understand what form the rewards will take. Crowns may symbolize increased responsibility. To some the words will be uttered, "Enter thou into the joy of thy Lord." Whatever the rewards may be, we are fools to do anything but cherish the thought of winning them.

A Mark of the Spirit

When Christ was on earth his presence provoked extreme devotion in some and equally extreme resentment in others. The mass of people was swayed between the two extremes—sometimes blindly enthusiastic and at other times blindly hostile. It was said of the Apostle Paul that wherever he went in the Mediterranean basin there was *either* a riot *or* a revival.

Wherever the Spirit of God is present in power, people react. At times the reaction will be hostile. But if it is, we are commanded to rejoice at such evident proof that "the spirit of glory and of God rests upon you." Nowadays the only reaction we anticipate as a result of the Spirit's presence is mass conversions. *It never occurs to us that per-*

secution may equally well indicate God's power.

Peter is very specific, however. The suffering he refers to is suffering "for the name of Christ" (1 Pet. 4:13). Christians sometimes suffer because of their arrogance or stupidity. Not all suffering is Christian suffering.

How then should a Christian react when persecution comes? We have already seen that he must live inoffensively. He must never merit punishment for bad behavior. We have also seen that he must do what he can to avoid persecution. He will have to take some risks of course. But as a basic principle he must assume that a living and active witness is better than a dead one.

Many years ago I visited Eastern Europe. I was moved by the love among the Christians whom I met and whom I was helping with Christian literature. Part of their activities were underground; a number of Christians had been imprisoned for carrying out certain activities (baptism, for example) disapproved of by the Government. What moved us most was the courage of some of the older women who would spend their afternoons distributing Christian literature. This was, of course, forbidden. To escape detection they would get on a street car, quickly check the passengers with experienced eyes, distribute literature, give a brief public testimony and alight at the next stop. From time to time one would be caught and sentenced to a period in jail. The fun of the game might appeal to the "cops and robbers" instinct in us, but for these women it was a serious way of life. But they used their wits to escape trouble (as we did ourselves).

Ethical problems raise their heads when the church or some of its activities is driven underground. What ought

I to have done when my Christian friends asked me to arrange for them to have more literature printed for them *bearing a pre-revolutionary date*? (I didn't, but I think I would do so now.) How is one to understand Paul's and Peter's admonitions to be obedient to civil authorities (Rom. 13:1-7; 1 Pet. 2:13-17)?

Clearly there are times when the claims of Caesar and those of Christ clash. It is the duty of Christians at such times to obey God rather than men. Peter and John were clear about this (Acts 4:15-20). The problems arise where it is less easy for us to know the will of God. Though this book is hardly the place to discuss the ethics of Christian underground resistance, we must recognize that there are certain imperatives for the Christian which *no* earthly ruler has the right to interfere with. Blessed is the Christian who has the courage to defy authority under such conditions and the wisdom to avoid getting caught.

And if you do get caught? If you are brought to trial?

Christians experience a number of reactions when they are apprehended for the sake of Christ. Almost all experience extreme anxiety—even fear. This is normal. Others are overwhelmed with self-doubt and a sense of guilt. Prison officers know how to play with devilish skill on the fears and doubts of Christian prisoners. A Christian will find himself asking: "Did I do right? Was I perhaps being too proud? Is the Lord trying to teach me a lesson? Have I not been irresponsible to my family? What will happen to my wife and children? Will my parents be harassed?" The world looks very different from the inside of a prison.

Yet if ever a Christian must be firm in suffering, it is

after he is captured. Two things he must never cease to do—two things that are closely related. First he must not give way to a sense of guilt or shame, but must praise and glorify God with his heart and, when he has a chance, with his mouth and lungs. (Paul and Silas unintentionally produced a midnight earthquake when they sang praises in prison.) I trust that most people who read these words never go to prison. But should you go for Christ's sake, trample false shame and guilt under your feet. Lift your head up high. Smile. Treat your jailors with courtesy. Above all praise and worship God.

The second thing to do is deliberately to entrust your fate to a faithful Creator (1 Pet. 4:19). He opens prison doors and has done so repeatedly in the ancient and modern world alike. At other times he has a purpose in keeping his servants locked up. Paul who was miraculously delivered from prison in Lystra seems not to have been in Rome. Yet from Rome came several of the Epistles. John Bunyan's greatest writing was done in jail.

And if death should await you, have no fear. Entrust your soul to him. You will be uplifted and empowered in a way that will cause men around you to shake their heads in wonder.

The
Pearl
Merchant

4

Your pulse may beat more quickly when you imagine what you would do if times become difficult. But as I write, times are not difficult. We enjoy freedom unparalleled in history. What then does it mean to take up your cross when little risk is involved in following Jesus? Does his teaching about the cross have meaning only when secret police pound doors at midnight?

No indeed. If you would follow Jesus, your whole view of life must change. You must look at the world through the eyes of Christ. Then things which once mattered greatly will cease to matter. Other things you once thought of no consequence will seem paramount to you.

But how does one look through the eyes of Christ? What is this changed orientation? Let me stress that its *essense* is *positive* not negative. I hope this will grow clearer as you read on. Christians have made serious mistakes down the ages by failing to grasp the positive emphasis of commitment. Even the term "sacrificial living" conjures up visions of hollow-cheeked earnestness. Its emphasis lies on doing without. It is as though the more you do without, the more spiritual your brand of Christianity is.

This "negative" view represents part of the truth. What we are going to talk about will indeed involve "going without." But as we shall see, self-denial is less than half the story. Indeed it is a serious distortion of the truth to stress the negative at the expense of the positive—the losses rather than the gains. It undermines the gospel of God's grace.

It does more than distort truth. It presents formidable spiritual hurdles for the person who seeks to put it into practice. You see, if you consciously deny yourself something you like, you find yourself battling an exalted view of your own spirituality. Your struggle is complicated by the fact that you have indeed done (as you see it) something virtuous. So something within you demands recognition. You can tell yourself as many times as you like that you "only did it by God's grace" or that it was "God's work within" you and not your own work at all. The fact of the matter is that it *is* your work. Though you were sincere in your sacrifice, it may well have represented self-effort, self-effort you are trying to palm off on the Holy Spirit in your futile struggle to stay humble.

You will also find it hard not to blame and criticize people who seem less dedicated than you. Naturally you don't want to be a Pharisee, so you will do your best to suppress critical feelings. But you won't be able to help them. They arise from a mistaken notion of what it is to follow Christ closely.

The Way of the Cross

Perhaps I had better begin negatively myself and start by saying what the Way of the Cross is *not*.

The Way of the Cross is not a denial of the value of intellectual activity. Some Christians say to me, "We don't believe in higher education. It is worldly." But it is not higher education that is worldly, only ambitions of academic glory. In Christ's army scholars and carpenters march shoulder to shoulder. No calling gets a higher rating than any other. It is our motive in pursuing the calling, whether academic or manual, that matters.

The Way of the Cross is not a denial of the value of artistic expression. Insofar as man's nature is corrupt, his creativity can be put to corrupt uses. Had you been a Hebrew in Joshua's day you would have had to destroy pictures and statues you captured in battle. You would have destroyed them because you were vulnerable to raw idolatry and demonism. You lived in an age in which the belief in evil deities and in their dwelling in images was strong. Certain spoils of war (with or without artistic merit) would be a serious hazard to you. So you would destroy them. Modern archaeologists and art historians might weep over the "priceless" treasures lost to posterity, but your responsibility at that point in history was to preserve something of greater value for posterity—the knowledge of the one true God, who did not dwell in images made by men. The loss of archaeological artifacts was a small price to pay to keep that of far greater worth.

Whether every puritanical assault upon the visual arts was justified, I cannot say. I raise the point because many devoted Christians for one reason or another have seen all artistic expression as suspect except the composition of "Christian" music, hymn writing, the writing of Christian novels and such. Without realizing it they measure spirituality in terms of cultural and artistic impoverishment, which is hardly what God intended.

The One whose creative genius gave us the awesome spectacle of stellar galaxies and the fragile beauty of snow crystals and orchids made us to be, like him, creators too. The danger of art is that we begin to worship artistic expression itself, instead of receiving it thankfully from his hands or giving it to him in worship. And that danger we must always watch.

Therefore you will not be sharing Christ's sufferings by putting your Beethoven records away forever (if Beethoven is what you like) unless there is a good reason for you to do so.

The Way of the Cross is not a denial of the rightness of pleasure. God invented pleasure. God gave it to man. The devil only taught man how to misuse it; he adulterated pleasure with evil, making it *sinful* pleasure. But the fact that men abuse pleasure is no reason for men of God to abandon it—leaving the impression that pleasure is essentially the devil's concession.

Pleasure must never become *lust.* Lust is born when pleasure becomes an end in itself, or when pursuing pleasure becomes more important to you than obeying God.

Christians find it hard to hold this truth in balance. It is so much easier to label certain pleasures evil, to say, for example, that sex apart from intended procreation is evil; that movies, novels, dancing, alcohol, tobacco, secular music are taboo; but that playing orchestral arrangements of pretty hymn tunes is virtuous and spiritual. It simplifies the whole question. And on the face of it the approach seems sound. So much in the movies, for instance, is not only garbage but *evil* garbage.

But we pay a price for such simplistic thinking. If all we were to sacrifice was the enjoyment of God-given delights, the price would be small. However, to the degree that we see our faith in negative terms we will, wittingly or unwittingly, so present it. Worse still, whatever we preach to the contrary, we will feel deep down inside us that if we observe the cardinal no-no's of evangelicalism we are being faithful followers of Christ. In fact, our lives may be empty not only of pleasure but also of godliness. Satan will then have gained a major victory in us.

Soldiers in war time must forego pleasure not because pleasure is evil (though some pleasures are) but because more pressing claims demand their attention. They may spend bitter months hungry, thirsty, eyes sore with wakefulness, dressed in foul-smelling clothes, feet blistered and limbs craving rest.

Yet their leaders know the value not only of food and rest but of recreation. They see to it that men are given furloughs with an opportunity for the pleasures they have been denied.

Christians are called to warfare. The times we live in will not be normal until Christ returns to reign. Pressing duties demand that we endure hardships and forego pleasure.

Yet at times our Heavenly Captain will heap upon us not only spiritual delights but, because we have physical bodies, physical delights as well. As followers of Christ we are not called to pursue pleasure but to follow our Leader. Yet we need not be discomfited by the showers of delight he occasionally surprises us with, even in times of war.

So far I have been explaining what the Way of the Cross is *not*. Since I have pleaded with you to see it in positive not in negative terms, it is time I did so myself. In positive terms the Way of the Cross is (1) the discovery of incomparable treasure at the cost of everything else in life and (2) the discovery of freedom at the price of selling myself into slavery.

The Incomparable Treasure

"The kingdom of heaven is like a treasure hidden in a field, which a man found and covered up; then *in his joy* he goes and sells all that he has and buys that field" (Mt. 13:44).

No details are given in this story except for the man's emotional state. He has discovered treasure buried in a field. How did he find it? Was he employed by the owner of the field? We do not know.

We know only three things. He covered the treasure up; he was delirious with joy; he was so excited that he sold everything he possessed in order to buy the field.

Here is a picture of reckless sacrifice, of wild abandonment of all a man possesses. Yet it is clearly not so much a picture of *renunciation* as it is of *re-evaluation*.

Up to this point in his life the man has doubtless valued his possessions highly. Like all of us he would have clung to them and only parted with them under exceptional circumstances. He might have lent to a neighbor in distress or sold something to help a close friend or relative. But by and large his life has consisted in the abundance of the things he possessed.

It is only when he discovers buried treasure that his perspective changes. Suddenly his possessions look cheap and paltry. A joy is rising in him and an excitement that makes him sweat and tremble. There may have been momentary regret about a cherished piece of furniture or a family heirloom. But it is only momentary. The choice he faces lies between his worthless bits and pieces and the field with buried treasure. There is nothing *noble* about his sacrifice. There would, on the other hand, be something incredibly stupid about not making it. Anyone but a fool would do exactly as the man did. Everyone will envy him his good fortune and commend him not on his spiritual character but on his common sense.

What I have called "his miserable bits and pieces" are the things of this life to which we naturally cling—money, property, cars, comforts, prestige, a good job. *Jesus is not telling us that we must sacrifice all our possessions to inherit heavenly treasure*, only that if we were to grasp what glories he has for us we would realize how silly we are to *cling* to such rubbish.

But we must be honest with ourselves. How important to us are possessions and ambitions? How real are heavenly treasures? We are like the man with the muckrake in the House of Interpreter in John Bunyan's *Pilgrim's Progress*, so absorbed with straws and rags that we fail to see the glorious crown extended to us.

There is a magnificent insanity about the parable that follows (Mt. 13:45). It has to do with a pearl freak—a merchant whose hobby was pearls. One day he evidently came across a pearl to end all pearls. You can imagine the quick intake of his breath, his staring eyes, the licking of his dry lips, the anxious inquiry about price, the haggling, the pondering of the tremendous cost of the pearl. You can also imagine him returning home and looking over the rest of his pearl collection. With shaking hands he would pick them up one by one and drop them into a soft leather pouch. Not only pearls but house, slaves, everything went so that the one pearl might become his.

And then, bereft of everything but a big pearl—what would the fool do? You can't eat pearls. In my mind is a picture of the crazy merchant sitting in a miserable hovel, his glowing eyes feasting on his pearl and his fingers gently caressing it. Crazy? Perhaps he is the one sane person among us.

It all depends on whether the pearl was worth it. We see at once that treasure in heaven would be worth it. Why then are we so quick to opt for earthly treasure and so slow to be obsessed with the heavenly? Perhaps it is because we *do not believe in heavenly realities*. They represent a celestial cliché in our minds, but no more. Basically you see, it is *faith* that makes us step lightheartedly along the Way of the Cross—not a spirit of sacrifice but faith that the next life *is* important, that Jesus *is* preparing a place on high.

The Way of the Cross is a magnificent obsession with a heavenly pearl, beside which everything else in life has no value. If it were a case of buying it, we would gladly sell all we had to do so.

But we could not buy heavenly treasure. It is not for sale. The point of the parable is that having caught a glimpse of the treasure we count all else of no value and pursue it.

Again and again in my life I have had to face choices. At one stage in my life it was English literature or Jesus. Though I was a medical student, I had a passion for literature. I even tried to collect first editions of Victorian novelists. I read late into the night, so late that I would be no use the next day. Good literature was an escape for me. I was not reading it as it should be read but drugging my mind in soporific clouds of words.

But God had shown me something of his own treasures and my heart craved them. In some dim way I perceived that my weakness for fiction interfered with my capacity to follow Christ. So I packed all the 18th- and 19th-century novelists and poets into a great crate and gave them to a friend who was majoring in English.

I was left with a sense of relief and gratitude. I have never questioned the sanity of that decision. Today, books are crammed untidily on all my bookshelves and litter every room in my house. They no longer hinder me as they once did.

I suppose the choice I made was a sacrifice. Yet I saw it more in terms of what I longed for more—my pearl.

Choices facing us may be comparatively trivial as well as great. The same principle holds. Once when I was on a winter holiday—a well earned one—an idea gripped me as I lay sunning on the beach. I had paper and pen with me, so I rolled over and began to write. A breeze was fluttering and tearing the loose pages I held down on the sand. The sun's caressing warmth turned into a head-aching glare. My position was uncomfortable. It would be much more sensible to go to my hotel room if I wanted to write. But I wanted a sun-tan to prove I had been on a winter holiday. I could not have it both ways. It was writing or tan. I chose writing.

My choice was not virtuous. It was simply a matter of what I wanted more. There were no "oughts" about it, though my choice may say something about my value system.

The Paradox of Freedom through Slavery

That choice and similar choices have left me thankful because they have begun to set me free. For to be free means to be released from being torn in two directions at once. It means to have one passion only—one pearl of great price—rather than half a dozen. Let me quote to you a letter written by an American communist in Mexico City, a letter breaking his engagement with his fiancée.

> We communists suffer many casualties. We are those whom they shoot, hang, lynch, tar and feather, imprison, slander, fire from our jobs and whose lives people make miserable in every way possible. Some of us are killed and imprisoned. We live in poverty. From what we earn we turn over to the Party every cent which we do not absolutely need to live.
>
> We communists have neither time nor money to

go to movies very often, nor for concerts nor for beautiful homes and new cars. They call us fanatics. We are fanatics. Our lives are dominated by one supreme factor—the struggle for world communism. We communists have a philosophy of life that money could not buy.

We have a cause to fight for, a specific goal in life. We lose our insignificant identities in the great river of humanity; and if our personal lives seem hard, or if our egos seem bruised through subordination to the Party, we are amply rewarded—in the thought that all of us, even though it be in a very small way, are contributing something new and better for humanity.

There is one thing about which I am completely in earnest—the communist cause. It is my life, my business, my religion, my hobby, my sweetheart, my wife, my mistress, my meat and drink. I work at it by day and dream of it by night. Its control over me grows greater with the passage of time. Therefore I cannot have a friend, a lover or even a conversation without relating them to this power that animates and controls my life. I measure people, books, ideas and deeds according to the way they affect the communist cause and by their attitude to it. I have already been in jail for my ideas, and if need be I am ready to face death. If the letter fails to stir you, you may already have begun to die. Like a traveler lost in a blizzard, unaware your body freezes in a snowbank, you are drifting to sleep.

But if your heart beats more quickly—be glad. You have hope of a more bracing life than the one most of us live. For Christ did not call you to suburbia and a mortgage but to a gibbet and a crown of glory.

The unknown communist in Mexico City startles us into seeing how trivial our lives are. We may not share his opinions. We may be appalled, even, at the abandon with which he hurls all that is dear to him into the crushing presses of a political machine. Yet we are glad to see a man who is willing to commit his all and even to die for what he believes in, however wrong he may be.

As you read the letter, you also feel he has been set free. Having broken from the possessions that clutter our own lives, he is consumed by a passion that despises both prudence and pleasure. For the time, at least, lusts that plague the rest of us seem to hold no attraction for him. Yet it is not the sternness of his renunciation that comes through, so much as an exhilarating sense of freedom.

His freedom has nothing to do with his political ideology. It has to do with his being a man, even a fallen man, released from lesser passions by pursuit of a greater. It is a freedom that may have awakened an echo in your own heart as you read his letter. For you were not created, much less redeemed, to sell your heritage for a mess of pottage. You have been called to a still more radical commitment than his and to gamble your life on higher stakes.

"If any man would come after me," Jesus again tells you, "let him deny himself and take up his cross daily and follow me" (Lk. 9:23).

The cross symbolizes your willingness to die if need be, or to give up all else for the surpassing glory of following it. Jesus calls you to pick it up and heave it over your back in the same way he carried his own cross—not in your lapel or round your neck but over your shoulders. It may look rough and heavy as you stare at it on the ground, but you will be surprised to find how light it feels as you bear it. And it will mark you in the eyes of demons, men and angels as one who despises humiliation and who deliberately chooses the company of the One from whom the world hides its face.

For the popular Christ and the true Christ are two different Christs. There is the watered-down Christ, remolded to please the masses. You may stand with *that* Christ and please as many people as he does. But the real Christ does not aim to please men so much as to love them and to glorify the Father. Jesus' truth pierced men's consciences; his love frightened and alienated them, while his relentless pursuit of the Father's glory threatened the institutions they upheld. They could not tolerate his continued existence and so they murdered him.

"If anyone serves me," Jesus once said, "he must follow me; and where I am, there shall my servant be also" (Jn. 12:26).

To stand where he stands, to walk in his steps means necessarily that you run the gauntlet of the attitudes that still slumber in men's hearts, attitudes you will awaken the moment you step after him. He wants you to understand this clearly before you make your choice. For to choose to follow him will mean you must say, as Paul said, "I do not account my life of any value nor as precious to myself" (Acts 20:24). You will have to place on the table your career, your money, your affections, your ambitions, your plans, your hobbies and your very life, and say, "It hurts me to place these here, but I know you can replace them a hundredfold. Let them be disposed of as they may—returned to me or lost forever. Their fate will not influence my choice. I want to follow you wholly." To do this is to be released from the chains that enslave men everywhere. It is also to take up your cross and to replace a heavy burden with a light one. It is to be set free.

One night when I was sixteen I was too excited to sleep. For the first time I saw the years of my life as a lump sum. Whereas many people spend their lives a few weeks at a time, squandering life aimlessly on whatever would catch their attention, I wanted to use the total sum of my years to purchase something big. Exciting fantasies swept over the screen of my imagination. Then in a moment of wonder and gratitude it occurred to me that I could hand my years in their entirety to Christ, to be disposed of in whatever way he chose. I knelt by my bed and did so.

My decision was not a noble one. In part at least it was based on self-interest. Yet he mercifully took me at my word and brought me back to that same decision repeatedly. I did not realize at the time that there was nothing mechanical about the contract between us. I supposed that having handed my years to him I would have no further say in the matter, and that automatically he would take the years from me, since they were his.

And so they were. My years truly belonged to him, and I had wholeheartedly acknowledged the fact. But I found I was still the administrator of them. Since they came to me one at a time, indeed one *day* at a time, I could only pay my debt in small installments. Jesus understood this when he said, "Let him . . . take up his cross *daily* and follow me." And this meant that the impulsive choice of a moment on a hot August night had to become the choice of every moment that followed. One act of my will had to become its continuous attitude. Two of those choices I have already described.

Happily Christ wanted to set me free even more than I wanted to *be* set free. And though like everyone around me I failed all too often to pay him what I owed, he pursued me relentlessly, teaching me in the thousands of small choices that I made how freedom could be found.

"If the Son makes you free, you will be free indeed" Jesus once stated (Jn. 8:36).

Is there any difference between the kind of freedom Jesus gives and the freedom the young communist seemed to experience in Mexico City? Do they share the same essential qualities? Both after all consist of being set free from petty enslavements to one great enslavement—an enslavement that liberates because I am doing what I want to do.

Let me say one more important thing about freedom: Freedom does not consist in doing what I want to do but in doing what I was designed to do. If I do what I want to do, I wind up not liking what I do. What at first promises liberty turns out to be a more onerous slavery.

You fling yourself with wild abandon to serve an ideology, and at first it feels like the most heady liberty you have ever known. But the high subsides. The sense of liberty goes. In the end the grim, dreary enslavement seems no better than the enslavement to your former selfish whims.

It matters little whether the ideology is communist or Christian. Many evangelical Christians find themselves enslaved to a hideous mixture of dogma, spiritual cliché and psychological technique. They are enslaved to a semi-Christian ideology rather than to a Person.

Do not misunderstand me. I do not underestimate the importance of truth. It is just that man was not designed to serve a theory—even a true theory. Theories enslave.

The Truth is a Person. Jesus alone gives freedom to human beings. He knows what he designed our beings for. He knows where true freedom exists for us. And he has infinite patience in teaching us, lesson by lesson, how to be free.

"Come to me," he invites us, "all who labor and are heavy-laden, and I will give you rest. Take my yoke upon you, and learn from me; for I am gentle and lowly in heart, and you will find rest for your souls. For my yoke is easy, and my burden is light" (Mt. 11:28-30).

The Loyalty That Calls for Hatred

5

What happens to your relationship with other people when you commit your life to Christ?

Every one who acknowledges me before men, I also will acknowledge before my Father who is in heaven; but whoever denies me before men, I also will deny before my Father who is in heaven.

Do not think that I have come to bring peace on earth; I have not come to bring peace, but a sword. For I have come to set a man against his father, and a daughter against her mother, and a daughter-in-law against her mother-in-law; and a man's foes will be those of his own household. He who loves father or mother more than me is not worthy of me; and he who loves son or daughter more than me is not worthy of me; and he who does not take his cross and follow me is not worthy of me. He who finds his life will lose it, and he who loses his life for my sake will find it. (Mt. 10:32-39).

Why do you transgress the commandment of God for the sake of your tradition? For God commanded, "Honor your father and your mother," and, "He who speaks evil of father or mother, let him surely die." But you say, "If any one tells his father or his mother, What you would have gained from me is given to God [i.e., 'I have given to Christian work the support I used to give to you'], he need not honor his father." So, for the sake of your tradition, you have made void the word of God. (Mt. 15:3-6)

If you commit yourself to Jesus Christ, you automatically change every other relationship in your life. When he becomes supreme to you, other people slip into different places. Those nearest you may become alienated. Those whom you once abhorred will become dear and intimate. The question of future marriage assumes a new solemnity. The re-evaluation and reorientation that follow commitment apply not only to values, but also to people.

The Paradox of Love and Hate
Yet when we examine the words of Jesus, we discover paradoxes. His statements on the subject at first seem confusing and contradictory. We are told to honor and respect our parents. Jesus vigorously condemns making God's work an excuse for ignoring parents' financial needs (Mt. 15:3-6). Yet he tells us that if we follow him we

must "hate" those nearest to us (Lk. 14:25-26). What does his teaching mean? Is it consistent?

Before we try to answer these questions, let us notice that the Bible is just as confusing about other relationships. Friendships can be dangerous. The godly man does not walk in the counsel of the ungodly; he does not stand in the way of sinners (Ps. 1:1). Repeatedly we are warned against friendship with evildoers. Yet in strange contrast we find Jesus himself eating with tax gatherers, prostitutes and sinners. As a physician seeks out the sick, so the Savior sought out sinners. And he urged his followers to do the same.

How do we explain the apparent contradiction? Does the Christian, perhaps, never truly *befriend* a non-Christian but approach him as a fisherman lures a fish or a salesman a likely prospect? The idea is abhorrent to most of us. Would Jesus, the great Fisher of Men, regard sinners with so calculating an eye? Does he not rather, like the Good Samaritan, feel his heart moved with compassion?

The difficulty begins to resolve itself when we realize that there are two elements in our feeling for someone else. I want my friend to like me, and I also want to show kindness for him; there is my longing that he will understand me and there is my concern to understand *him*. Both elements—the need element and the giving element—are present in any relationship, but they show themselves in different ways and may exist in different proportions.

Jim, an immature husband of 40, weeps bitterly when his wife walks out. He admits he has been a poor husband,

"But God knows I love her. I can't live without her." As we talk, it becomes evident that he is still highly critical of his wife. A stream of bitter words pours through his lips as he describes the woman he says he loves. "She has no heart. She can't leave! How can she do this to me? She's mean. She has no feelings."

"I love her." "She has no heart." What is he saying? He's telling me that he wants this woman to be nice to him; to come back, hold his hand, darn his socks, make his meals and go to bed with him. He has the same kind of feeling for her as he had for his momma and his teddy bear.

But he has no compassion for her. He does not grieve over the pain she endures. He has little concern for her happiness, only for his own.

How different were the feelings of the father of the prodigal son (Lk. 15). Knowing full well the difficulties and dangers the boy faced, he still gave him his part of the legacy and let him leave home. He concealed his own aching heart and sent the boy on his way. "Need love" there was. The old man must have watched daily from the house top, straining his aging eyes, yearning for the fruit of his body. But he had let the boy go. Therefore he must also have perceived the needs and longings in the boy's own heart and suppressed his personal yearnings for the sake of his son.

We can now understand the apparent contradictions in Scripture. For we associate with people for different reasons.

Joe, an insecure adolescent from a fundamentalist home, yearns for the approval and admiration of his

peers. If they smoke, he must smoke more. If they copu-
late (or say they do), his stories of conquest must outrank
theirs. When his letters to his girl friends fall into his
parents' hands, they sit down, shaking and weak at the
appalling obscenity and evil they read.

Yet these are his friends, he protests. They understand him. They're his buddies. Sure, he shouldn't have
said those things. Joe was mostly bragging anyway. But
his friends—he can't give up his friends.

Why? Because he needs to feel wanted and accepted
and at last he has found a group that admires him. Does
he talk to them of Christ? He hangs his head. "Well, they
know you guys are religious. I told them I have to go to
church. But they don't mind. They're pretty decent
about it."

At this point friendship with the world is indeed
enmity with God. For Joe's actions are based on his
pathetic need to be accepted and admired. Much as we
may sympathize, we know he is selling his birthright too
cheaply. Millions of men and women have abandoned
the treasures of heaven and run downhill with the crowd
for the same pitiable reason. Friendship with evildoers
under these circumstances is wrong and harmful.

All of us share Joe's problem in some degree. It affects
our relationship with those closest to us.

How does the Muslim convert feel when he is hounded
from home and village because he confessed Christ? He
need only retract his confession. He could even keep it
secret—and the family would welcome him into its bosom
again. No, he is not hating them as he is driven from their
midst. But a new love, greater than any love he has ever

before experienced, so grips his heart that even love of family can be called hate in comparison with that love. Yet he weeps as he goes and his heart is heavy.

And what of you when family and friends mock you?

Once again, Jesus never permits us to fail in our responsibilities. He insists we give love and affection to our parents, spouses, children or anyone else who may have a claim on us. Even money given to God's work when it is given at the expense of our needy relatives is a sin against God's holy law (Mt. 15:3-6). The Apostle Paul calls someone who fails to provide for his family "worse than an infidel" (1 Tim. 5:8, AV). Jesus on the cross was still concerned about the welfare of the mother he left behind.

No. To "hate" one's family has a very different meaning. For family, especially a warm and happy family, comforts and cherishes its members. To hate one's family means to be so committed to Christ that however much it costs me to be away from that circle, I must cut myself ruthlessly from its comfort and follow him barefoot on rocky pathways. It means that I must embrace my wife, and she me, as we say weeping together, "It won't be long, honey. It's for Jesus' sake."

A Paradox and a Premonition

Hate?

Once I had a premonition that my wife and infant son would be killed in a flying accident. We were to travel separately from the U.S. to Bolivia, South America. She would fly via Brazil, Buenos Aires, then north to Bolivia. I was to visit Mexico, several Central American countries, Venezuela, Colombia and other countries, to strengthen

Christian work among students, before joining them in Bolivia.

The premonition came with sickening certainty just before we parted on the night of a wild snowstorm. I felt I was a cowardly fool as I drove away and saw Lorrie silhouetted in the yellow light of the doorway, surrounded by swirling snowflakes. Why didn't I go back and tell her I would cancel the flights? Why didn't I act on this foreboding?

Yet I felt a fool. I didn't believe in premonitions—and she would probably laugh. Besides I was late, I had to get to the place where I would spend the night before my early morning flight. Fear, shame, guilt, nausea, all boiled inside me during the miserable drive to my hotel. No conversation was possible with the man who was driving me.

In bed I tossed in misery. Of course I prayed. By faith I was going to have it licked. Faith? In the presence of so powerful a premonition? My mouth was dry. My limbs shook. God was a million miles away. The hours crawled by, each one a year of fear. Why didn't I get dressed, hire a car and go back to them?

"What's the matter? Can't you trust me?"

I was startled. Was God speaking?

"Yes, I'll trust you—if you promise to give them back to me."

Silence.

Then, "And if I don't promise? If I don't give them back to you, *will you stop trusting me?*"

Oh God, what are you saying? My heart had stopped and I couldn't breathe.

"Can you not entrust them to me in death as well as in life?"

Suddenly a physical warmth flowed through all my body. I think I wept a little. My words came tremblingly and weakly, "Yes, I place them in your hands. I know you will take care of them, in life or in death."

And my trembling subsided. Peace—better by far than martinis on an empty stomach—flowed over and over me. And drowsily I drifted off to sleep.

Hate them? How could I ever hate them? Yet by faith I had said in effect: I will do your will whatever it costs to me or them, and I will trust you.

Their plane crashed. Everyone on board was killed. But my wife had also had a premonition and cut their journey short, getting off the plane the stop before the tragedy occurred.

I am grateful for the way it worked out. But I didn't know beforehand that things would go as they did. And had it not worked out that way I would have grieved (God knows how I would have grieved), but I would *not* have regretted my decision to trust and to go forward.

This is what it means to follow Christ fully. This is the effect he wants to have on all our personal relationships, family members, fiancés, friends—whoever they may be. What of your own nearest and dearest? The fear that may hold you back is a fear of unbelief. But defy your fear and go forward. For to follow Christ fully means to take steps along the perilous pathway of trust, roped to the safest Guide in the universe.

Pilgrim,
Stranger,
Displaced Person

6

It would be a mistake to call Abraham a nomad. True, he adopted a nomadic lifestyle. But the difference between Abraham and neighboring tribesmen was that though Abraham had left a settled existence behind, he was looking ahead to a more permanent one. He was in search of a country where he and his descendants could live in peace.

The Homing Instinct

Abraham never saw his vision turn into reality. Though he found the country he was looking for, he never possessed it. His descendants did. But hundreds of years were to pass before even they inherited the promise. Meanwhile Abraham remained a wandering stranger in the country he had intended to settle. He is described variously as "pilgrim," "sojourner," "stranger." Were he a child of the twentieth century, we might call him a "displaced person."

Abraham is thus the prototype of the follower of Jesus. We do not live in tents as Abraham the sojourner did. We may not even be called to "live out of a suitcase" as some of our modern brothers and sisters. Yet if we are serious about following Christ we share Abraham's outlook.

We do not "belong." We are temporary residents only. Our real home is not immediately available, but we refuse to settle permanently anywhere else. We are "pilgrims and strangers."

We have not chosen impermanence as a preferred lifestyle. We are not nomadic. A nomad thinks only of the next temporary pasture. Deep within us, however, is a longing for our true home. It is this longing that characterizes the people of God. They do not belong to this world *because they do belong somewhere else*.

Nor do they long for home because they want to escape from difficult circumstances. Such a longing would be pathological and escapist. The escapist is at home nowhere. Just as the nomad is thinking of the next pasture, so the escapist is always fleeing the previous one.

The urge to find a home is a deep human instinct. Something of its pathos and beauty has been seen during our century in the return of the descendants of Abraham to the earthly home of their forefathers. The passion, the pain, the sufferings and the struggle, however ugly they may be in themselves, testify to the tenacity of the homing instinct.

If we judge by the people who are in modern Israel, we can make a generalization. People from areas of persecution feel the urge more keenly than people who are prosperous, settled and comfortable. Thus U.S. Jews may subscribe most of the finances to float Israel, but U.S. Jews are much less likely to tear up their roots and *live* there than are Jews persecuted for being Jewish. A New York and a Tel Aviv Jew are very different people.

There is a parallel in the church. Christians who are prosperous and comfortable on earth may give money generously to Christian work but usually find it hard to think of heaven as *home*. It is one thing to speak piously about dying as "going home," but quite another to "put our money where our mouth is." Tragically, many who talk piously about "home" display little evidence of longing to be there. Home in Florida is more attractive. Tension exists between home on earth and home in heaven, and there are practical ways in which we can discover where our real interest lies.

Where Your Treasure Is

Psychoanalysts talk about *cathexis*. Cathexis means (approximately) emotional investment. To *cathect* something *heavily* means that your emotional life is pretty tangled up with whatever you cathect. The question that faces every Christian is this: Given that we are less concerned about heaven the more we are wrapped up with earth; and given that the more wrapped up in heaven we are the less anxious we will be about our earthly home—how much cathexis do we invest in mansions in the skies? I grow weary of the evangelical cliché that describes people who are "so heavenly minded that they are no earthly good." Years have passed since I met anyone fitting the description. By and large my Christian acquaintances are too earthly minded to be any *heavenly* good. And this should concern us far more.

A little while ago we were planning to make a move to another country. Our plans affected our outlook and behavior. They influenced our feelings about the house we lived in. We looked at our house through the eyes of a prospective buyer and were no longer concerned about making it more comfortable for ourselves.

The move affected our buying habits. We stopped looking for good buys on winter clothes (there was no winter where we were going). We found ourselves making do with gadgets that were wearing out rather than buying new ones. We put up with many minor inconveniences. I weathered a Manitoba winter in a thin, cheap winter coat.

We were not being virtuous. We wanted to make sure we had money enough to make a good start in the country we were going *to*. We were reducing our cathexis in Canada and increasing it in the Caribbean. Our interest in Canada was diminishing while our interest in the Caribbean was growing.

Jesus was talking about exactly the same thing when he urged us to lay up treasure in heaven. His words blast our self-deception away: *"Where your treasure is, there will your heart be also"* (Mt. 6:21)—a simple way to say that his followers would cathect heaven more than earth.

Jesus knew the tug of war in our hearts between heavenly and earthly homes. He knew our struggle between money-love and heavenly treasure. He told us we needed "a single eye." He warned that without that single (or "sound") eye, we would grope in terrible inner darkness (Mt. 6:22-23). Torn perpetually in two directions, we could never see clearly the issues confronting us. We would go through life confused and bewildered, plagued with a sense of guilt and alienation, and never sure where we were going.

It is far easier for the man who makes up his mind to pursue money and money alone. At least he knows where he is going. Provided he is not hampered by qualms of conscience or the pull of other aims and ideals, he too will have a single eye. He cuts a less pathetic figure than the Christian who straddles the fence.

It would be simpler if Christians were called to vows of poverty. If we knew it was God's will that none of us own cars; that all of us were allowed precisely two sets of underwear, one set of outerwear and $50 a month rent, one pair of slippers and one pair of shoes, we would all know where we stood.

But Jesus does not make it that easy. His teaching about giving away a second suit to someone who has none is not an attempt to set maximum living standards. As a matter of fact, as any welfare officer knows, once you get into the "bag" of what you're entitled to and what you're not entitled to, you find many grey areas. More than that, instead of being focused on heaven, you do in fact become more "thing-centered" than ever. For instance, what do I do with my $50 rent allowance when the choice lies between an inconvenient hovel ten miles from work at $25 a month and a room nearby which is $52 a month?

Voluntary poverty has many subtle problems, and it can still leave a man a secret worshiper of mammon.

No One Can Serve Two Masters

Jesus wanted to set us free from mammon *in our hearts*. His second illustration makes this abundantly clear. "No one can serve two masters," he states categorically. "You cannot serve God and mammon" (Mt. 6:24). Mammon, in the context, seems to refer to *care* about material necessities. He is concerned, as he always is, with the inner struggle we all experience between things and God.

Quite often we speak of the "rat race." Rats may well enjoy (we have no means of knowing) the exercise wheels that adorn their cages. But to humans the wheel symbolizes the endless struggle of daily living with its depressing sense of never moving forward. It is difficult to avoid getting trapped in a rat race if one lives in the Western world. We are gripped by the delusion that if we earn a little more money we will be set free. But the carrot of better and finer toys dangles perpetually before our noses, so that we spend more than we earn. To his horror a man discovers that he is making $50,000 annually but that the goal of freedom is still another $20,000 or $30,000 away. Like a mirage in the desert, it has receded as he advanced.

A man may earn $100,000 and feel the bitterness of slavery in his soul. You will say, "If *I* earned that much I wouldn't feel enslaved," and will then proceed to tell me how you would go about freeing up your time. But if you are not free now with the income you earn, you will be no more free with fifty times as much. Freedom is an inner contentment with what you have. It means to covet only heavenly treasure.

Such an attitude frees you not only because you feel free psychologically, but because it frees your vision. It enables you to look at your life in a new way, so that you may discover, for instance, that you do not need to work the long hours you do but could spend more hours in direct involvement with the kingdom.

You may now begin to see why Jesus did not concentrate on precisely what possessions a man should have but rather on his need to decide between God and mammon. For the decision against mammon is a decision to say, "I am here only a little while. All I need is enough to keep myself and my dependents alive. If God should give me more (and he is a very bountiful God), I shall accept gladly what he provides. But I shall not pursue it or make myself a slave for more than I actually need. My real treasure is in heaven."

I can hear in my mind a background of voices using words like "practical," "realistic," "sense of proportion," "sense of responsibility." I am sure their unending chorus will continue till the close of time. Even when I hear the word "definition." ("How do you *define* the amount you need to stay alive? Are you talking about just keeping body and soul together or are things like health and education necessary?" and so forth), I refuse to rise to the bait. Once we get into definitions of that kind, we shall slowly become fascinated with the here and now. Things like "need" define themselves once our priorities are straightened out. "Need" at one point in time and space is not the same as in another. But who cares? What we are talking about is freedom from ambivalence, not about how many hairs make a beard.

Your Treasure in Heaven

I cannot leave this whole question, however, without discussing treasure in heaven. If there is an area I should be more explicit about, it is this. I have already confessed that I don't know what the treasure is. Obviously it is valuable to us hereafter. Just as obviously, it will not cause us the anxiety earthly investments do (Mt. 6:19-20). Securities belie their name. Banks and insurance companies will pass away. Precious metals have all through history been stolen. There is no such thing on earth as a *safe* investment—not even a *fairly* safe one. But heavenly treasure is guaranteed by the Name of Jehovah. It is of value. It is secure.

Yet how little importance we attach to it.

You see, to store up heavenly treasure takes *earthly time*—time that otherwise could be devoted to pursuing cars and carpets. This is the whole point in what Jesus is saying. And we reveal where our interest lies by the way we distribute our energies. Just as Roman Catholics in past years sought to buy heavenly favors with earthly cash, so evangelicals try to buy heavenly treasure by giving money to missions. You cannot buy heavenly treasure with dollars. The exchange rate is zilch. You have to labor for heavenly treasure just as you would for earthly rewards. The only difference is that the one labor is a joy and a delight while the other enslaves.

What exactly is the treasure? Scripture never says. In the parables, faithful stewards get to reign. The explicit teaching of Paul is, "If we endure [suffer with him], we shall also reign with him" (2 Tim. 2:12). Are the reward of reigning and "treasure" one and the same? Perhaps yes; perhaps no.

It is interesting to notice how different treasures affect people. Pearls, diamonds and gold are associated with piracy, theft, murder, holdups, anxiety, greed, cruelty, torture. The longing to possess them awakens unwholesome passions in men. What if the "treasure" were an increased capacity to appreciate Christ (as many commentators suggest)? Certainly a longing to know Christ in all his beauty has very different effects on Christians than the chance of making a million dollars.

Living the Examined Life

Look at yourself, my brother, my sister, in the mirror of Christ's Word. Ask the person you see in the mirror: "Where is my treasure? Where is my heart? Where do my real ambitions lie? Am I a child of the universe—or a true hybrid—someone who is now a child of eternity?"

Look hard at your mirror-image. Do not evade the eyes you see. They will tell you the truth; and you need to face the truth if you are to be freed. Deep in your heart you want to be set free, but you must look first at your chains.

> Our souls are held by what they hold;
> Slaves still are slaves in chains of gold;
> To whatsoever we may cling,
> We make it a soul-chaining thing;
> Whether it be a life, or land,
> And dear as our right eye or hand.[3]

Then struggle in your chains to Jesus. Ask him to strike them for you. Then pick them up and fling them into eternal fires. Declare before the unseen host of onlookers, "I am a citizen of heaven. I have one Lord and him only will I serve." As you do so you will experience what Charles Wesley describes:

My chains fell off,
My heart was free,
I rose, went forth,
And followed Thee.

How then do we labor for treasure in heaven? The theme recurs in the Gospels in both parables and plain teaching.

Two ideas seem paramount. One is that we have been given certain potential (time, opportunities, abilities, and so forth) which can be employed in the interest of the kingdom. Each of us is responsible to God to render to him from the potential that he has given us. The second and related idea is that according to how well we use the potential we will be given reward or treasure.

I have already pointed out that it is possible for many of us to free up our time to serve God, once we get our priorities sorted out. I know an insurance agent, for instance, who gives his summer months to Christian camps and lives on his winter earnings. Anyone who is his own boss can figure out a similar plan.

I am not saying that earning money is secular and that Christian camps constitute "true Christian service." Rather I am saying that many of us would find we had more time than we thought if we made less of a priority of money.

What is your own potential? What has God given you in time, in money, in physique, in natural gifts and in spiritual abilities? In what way can they be used for the kingdom and to what extent have you used this potential?

Have you used it at all today? This week? This past month? As you look back over the year, to what extent have you been living for God?

If your conscience troubles you, how soon can you act? At the end of your college year? When you get another job? When you get married?

Could you start now?

The Pathway of Faith

7

Re-evaluation, reorientation, freedom: They will
begin to take place in your life when you take a step. For
commitment is a journey, and as the Chinese proverb re-
minds us, the longest journey begins with the first step.
At this moment there may well be a specific decision you
can make which will constitute that first step. God knows
what that step is, and he wants to show it to you.

The First Step of Faith

In Abram's case, the first step was to leave the tiny
Chaldean settlement of Harran. Terah, his father, had
settled there years before on a pilgrimage that was never
completed. The whole family had started out for
Canaan. "Terah took his son Abram [and] his grandson
Lot . . . and they set out from Ur of the Chaldees for the

land of Canaan. But when they reached Harran, they settled there" (Gen. 11:31-32, NEB). They were still there when Terah, Abram's father, eventually died.

Abram had all the feelings you have. He would weep over his father's corpse. He would be fussed and humiliated over his inability to impregnate Sarai. He would be concerned about his responsibility to his nephew Lot. It was in the middle of sorrow, frustration and responsibility that God's call came, commanding him to set out again "to a country that I will show you."

Sorrow and frustration notwithstanding, there was comfort in Harran. Not only had the family made friends, but extended family connections held them in a comforting network. They would be familiar with the country, with the way of life, and would have a recognized place in the local society. Sacrifice would be involved if Abram were to follow God's word. He would leave his father's remains behind him. His responsibility for Lot's well-being would increase. He would need to find new pastures for his animals and perhaps to relearn the ways and customs of nomadic tribesmen.

God's call to Abram can therefore be seen as a call to make a radical step of commitment. And since the step involved a great cost, it would be a sacrificial commitment.

Yet are we to view the move as an example of sacrificial obedience or as a gamble of faith? For the word that came to him was, "I will make you into a great nation, I will bless you and make your name so great that it shall be used in blessings: . . . All the families on earth will pray to be blessed as you are blessed" (Gen. 12:2-3, NEB).

Look at it another way. In Harran lay obscurity and eventual oblivion. In the call of God lay an immortal destiny. In packing up his belongings and moving his family across the desert, Abram was taking the first step in what was to become the all-time classic life of faith. He was in addition to set in motion a stream of history which would change the Western world for three millenia, would allow Abram to contribute through his descen-dants more to modern music, drama, science and banking than any other man and would ensure that those same descendants would remain at the center stage of world history at the end of time. From his loins would spring not only kings and prophets but the redeemer of the world. It is impossible to estimate the effects on human history of Abram's decision to leave Harran.

But Abram had no means of foreseeing, let alone understanding Einsteinian physics, Rothsteinian banking or two thousand years of church history. He had but the word of God and the promise of a destiny. His decision to move out, sacrifice or no sacrifice, was essentially a gamble of faith. He trusted God that there were better things for him than lay in Harran.

I do not know what your Harran is. To leave it may be a less traumatic decision than Abram's. But in its way it will be just as momentous. It will be a step into freedom.

In the Caribbean I watched people catching monkeys by leaving peanuts inside a coconut shell tied to a tree. There was a hole in the coconut shell big enough for the monkey to insert its fingers and grab the nuts, but not big enough for it to withdraw a fist filled with them. Your first step into freedom may involve dropping a few peanuts. Which is it to be—peanuts or a destiny?

For Abram there were many more steps along the journey of faith/commitment. His faith, like your own, tended to be sporadic. His confidence in God's promise seemed to wax and wane, failing altogether in crises of humiliation and shame.

If Abram had anticipated a life of superficial excitement, or even of instant prosperity, he would have been disappointed. Soon after leaving Harran, the famine descended around him, famine so severe that he felt forced to move to Egypt. To go back to Harran was unthinkable, yet the choice to go south was a reluctant one.

Egypt spelled elegance, power and sophistication to Abram, all of which he found menacing. His fears coalesced into an obsession about Sarai, whose beauty had attracted comment wherever they had been. Female beauty was something Egyptians could appreciate. Would they perhaps seize her? Would his life be in danger because of her? Machismo played no part in his make-up. He may have felt little shame as he instructed her, "Tell them you are my sister. That way both of us will survive" (Gen. 12:13, NEB).

His fears proved realistic. Pharaoh's courtiers, anxious to advance in their master's eyes, were quick to see an opportunity of pandering to his well-developed sense of possession and his sensuality. Like the precocious little boys who tempt sailors in foreign ports with stories of their "beautiful girl" contacts, the courtiers hastened to pour exciting descriptions of Sarai's attributes into the ears of Pharaoh. Abram's "sister" was soon added to the royal collection. Everyone would be delighted—everyone, that is, except Abram and Sarai. And God.

For God had a large stake in the life of a man who would leave home and kindred on the basis of his promise. Abram's behavior may have been unmanly. From the twentieth century we cannot judge. Certainly the unheroic figure which he cuts contrasts strangely with the "giant-of-the-faith" portrait that is commonly painted of him.

But God moved in to rescue him. The plague that afflicted Pharaoh's household, the vision of God that awoke terror in Pharaoh's heart and the restoration of Sarai are now part of history. Abram was rewarded for his perfidy with vast increases in his herds and sent on his way ignominiously.

A Mingling of Mud and Marble

You can take heart from the incident. In discovering Abram's weaknesses you discover that you are in the same league with him. Greek heroes and Bible heroes are qualitatively different. You can only identify with Odysseus by playing Walter Mitty. But with Abram you can identify realistically. Abram, you see, was a little man who learned to make great decisions so that he eventually enacted a saga of faith/commitment. The fact that he also made a few despicable decisions en route merely shows us that he was not Homeric. He was human.

And how human! Patriarchal pitfalls are glossed over in sermons and books. We seem to have a need to see a Homeric rather than a godly Abram. We busily window-dress his story and make of it a sales display. We not only window-dress; we window-*shop*. We can admire, without having to buy what we see. Having window-dressed, we can indeed no longer afford to buy. The price is too high.

I want, in contrast, to sell you the human Abram, the Abram of the Egyptian affair and of the Hagar-Ishmael debacle. The Egyptian affair shows his susceptibility to fear. The Hagar incident shows his unbelief and his weakness in giving way too easily to Sarai.

Sarai was deeply disheartened that she could not become pregnant. All God's promises would be meaningless, of course, if Sarai didn't produce. You can't become the father of nations if you don't begin by being the father of one child. Sarai would see herself as a failure and a hindrance not only as a wife but also to the fulfillment of God's promise. In desperation she worked out a compromise and, according to local custom, offered her maid to Abram as a bed partner. Any child born to Hagar would be counted as Sarai's.

It was the kind of compromise we make ourselves. It is so easy to figure out *practical* ways by which we can make God's promises come true. The end and the means loom larger in our thinking than God does. Faith in God shrivels before uneasy rationalizations which when put into practice leave everyone concerned unhappier than they were before and, more important, alienated from God.

What made Abram go to bed with Hagar? Lechery may have made the decision easier but may equally well have played no part. A desire to placate Sarai was probably more important. We are told nothing of his feelings but the easy way in which he went along with her later plan to be rid of Hagar reveals his weakness. The whole story of the expulsion of mother and son (Abram's own son) into the inhospitable desert is a shocking revelation of Abram's weakness. Nor can there be much question that a disappointing sense of remoteness and unreality of God's promise took away the last resistance to his unhappy courses of action. He was called to walk in steps of faith, but the echo of the call seemed elusive and distant so that his steps faltered.

You are made, Abram, of the same shameful stuff we are made of ourselves. We are glad that the shabby details of your actions have been laid on the line. There was no other way we could know you share with us the mingling of mud and marble that make up a man.

And marble there is and was. The noble decision at Harran to gamble on the promises of an invisible God was a decision made many times over. Though the call could wax faint, it would break into his consciousness repeatedly and with renewed force and clarity. Caught up by the impelling word of God he would re-enact his Harran decision. Sometimes the word came after he had, in the absence of any strong assurance, acted as he knew he should. Then in the aftermath of the decision, as he stood and trembled at his own temerity, the comfort of reassurance would come.

Such was the case when he gave Lot the first choice of grazing land. The two men's herders had been at odds over grazing and water. Tensions were growing. As the senior family member as well as the more powerful of the two, Abram could easily have insisted upon some arrangement more advantageous to himself. Instead he told Lot to take his pick of available land. He himself would move family and flocks to whatever area Lot rejected.

Lot chose the best land. If someone offers you a plum, why not take it? And Abram held firmly to his agreement.

On the surface it was nothing more than a generous manner of working out a family problem. But it was more. God had promised the land to Abram. In offering grazing areas to Lot, Abram was opening the way for Lot to stake claims in the very area he himself hoped one day to possess. Was he being weak and muddle-headed, or was he demonstrating extraordinary faith in the promise? It seems to me that where family duty (remember, Abram had a responsibility towards Lot) and his own ambitions for the future came into conflict, he chose loyalty and trusted God to look after the consequences. My intuition is borne out by the fact that twice in the years that followed, Abram went out on a limb to rescue Lot. One occasion involved a hazardous rescue attempt, while another involved, as Abram saw it, jeopardizing his own relationship with God. Yet Abram risked his life, his future, and even God's favor to intervene on Lot's behalf. Abram might make mistakes. He might be too eager to please Sarai. Yet his attitude to Lot revealed his deep faith in God's promise.

The Last Step on the Way of the Cross

So far in this chapter I have tried to make a number of things clear. First, I have been careful to point out that Abram's sacrificial commitment to God is best seen not as sacrifice but first as a step, then as a journey of faith. Second, I have tried to show that there was nothing extraordinary about the man himself. He had serious flaws. Third and most important, Abram's journey of faith can only be understood if we see it as a response to the re-iterated call and repeated promises of God.

How that call and those promises came to him is imma-terial. Whether they came in the form of auditory voices or an inner conviction is actually beside the point. If God exists and if God wants to communicate with a man, he may choose any vehicle through which to communicate. Of one thing we may be sure. If God *wants* to get some-thing across he will. And the glory of the God of the Scriptures is that he longs to communicate—not only to an Abram but to all his servants. The story of Abram is recorded because it can be your story. God sees you, too, as his servant.

Two incidents stand out that reinforce the strange interaction between God's word and the faith of Abram (or Abraham as he was later named). The more disturb-ing of the two, and certainly the climax and the greatest turning point of his life, was the sacrifice of his promised son, Isaac.

Nowhere else in the Bible does God command human sacrifice. Indeed the sacrifice by parents of their off-spring is singled out as being abhorrent to God. Why did God command Abraham to do something he abhorred?

We must be clear on two points. Abraham would not share our modern feelings about human sacrifice. That is to say, it would present him with no *moral* problem. Whatever feelings of dread and sorrow he might struggle against, there would never occur to him the idea that human sacrifice was in itself evil. It was the accepted practice of his day. If it meant anything to him, it would signify a proof of devotion to his God.

The second point arises from this fact. Knowing how Abraham would view the command (that is, as an act of devotion) God, we read, *tested* Abraham. Would Abraham (not a man of the twentieth century, but a child of a dark age where the offering of one's children to God in sacrifice was the ultimate proof of love and trust) trust God enough to obey the command? Having waited years for the impossible—a child from his own and Sarah's bodies—could he trust God to keep the promise made at Harran, a promise repeated many times since?

Abraham's decision to sacrifice Isaac represents the last step of his journey. If we view it as a commitment, his commitment is now complete. If we view it as faith (where the true heart of the matter lies), his trust in God is great enough now to fly in the face of instinct and common sense. So much is he prepared to gamble on the word of God that he gets ready to plunge a knife into the body of his own boy, because "he considered that God was able to raise men even from the dead" (Heb. 11:19).

The knife was raised but God intervened. Abraham's bewildered eyes saw a living ram caught in a thicket beside him. His ears heard the now familiar voice telling him to release the ropes that bound his son to the altar. God's purpose was accomplished. He had taught a man to trust him.

And this is all he wants to teach you. Whether you hear him or not he is calling you. Tune out other clamoring sounds. In the depths of your spirit he waits to meet you. Let there be no doubt in your mind, he is going to extraordinary lengths to communicate with you.

Years before the climactic scene by the altar, God had spoken to Abraham in terms that Abraham could not possibly mistake. The local custom in making a contract called for an unusual ceremony. An animal would be divided in half and the two halves laid a few feet apart. Parties to the contract would walk between the divided remains of the animal. In doing so they were saying in symbol, "May my body be cut in half in the way this animal's body is, if I should betray my word and break my covenant." Such a contract was exceedingly solemn and binding.

Even before Abram's name was changed to Abraham, God made exactly this sort of covenant with him. Abram was instructed to take five living creatures (signifying the extreme solemnity of the occasion)—a heifer, a female goat, a ram, a dove and a pigeon, and to divide the animals (the heifer, the goat and the ram) in half, laying them according to the prescribed covenant ritual (Gen. 15:1-21).

At the time Abram had grave doubts about God's promise to him. His faith was low. Nevertheless he laid out the animals in the accepted manner and waited. Hours passed. Vultures descended from time to time to seize the dead flesh, and Abram was obliged constantly to drive them away. Slowly the sun went down, and as it did so a nightmare-like trance passed over Abram. Further revelations of God's will were made to him. Then in the darkness a glowing brazier and a flaming torch appeared, symbolizing the presence of God. Both the brazier and the torch passed between the divided halves of the dead animals. "To your descendants," the voice came, "I give this land," sealing the covenant in a manner that any nomad of that age would understand.

You say you wish God would go to such pains to speak to you?

Stand at Golgotha as the horror of darkness falls. Look at the God-man who hangs in extremis from a gibbet. Dare you demand further evidence of God's good will in his negotiations with you? The brazier and the torch have passed between the animals. God has committed himself. He has spoken the irrevocable word for your comfort and your assurance.

Perhaps you are waiting as the sun goes down. Perhaps vultures would snatch away the evidence that any contract exists between you and God.

Go to the Scriptures. Read in the Gospels all that took place. Christ's body was of human flesh and it was lifted up on a cross. The darkness actually descended. The veil in the temple was torn in two. These things happened and were recorded that you might know God has committed himself to anyone who trusts him. He has gone to great pains to assure you that the gamble of faith is no gamble; that your commitment, your sacrifice, your step of faith will represent an entry into a deeper relationship with himself. The cost to you is trivial. What he offers is of far greater value. But you must believe— enough to take some specific step.

If you are uncertain, be in no hurry to decide what that step is. Do not move from Harran in fevered panic. Wait before God in silence. Are there pressures and frustrations? Go within yourself to the tabernacle where God abides in stillness. Tell him you worship him. He will speak since he is more anxious to reach you than you are to be reached.

He is in fact already speaking. It is only necessary that you listen.

Notes
¹Samuel W. Gandy, "I Hear the Accuser Roar," *The Believers' Hymn Book* (London: Pickering and Inglis).
²Ibid.
³Arthur S. Booth Clibborn, "There Is No Gain."